GR
EXPEC

Original story by Charles Dickens
Retold by Julia Golding
Series Advisor Professor Kimberley Reynolds
Illustrated by Simon Bartram

OXFORD
UNIVERSITY PRESS

GW00746326

24260

NOt AR

Letter from the Author

I wrote my first story when I was about eight. It was about a tapestry that was a doorway into another world but somehow the characters ended up in space. After a spell as a British diplomat, then working for Oxfam, I now write stories full-time. I haven't yet returned to the solar system in my books but never say never! I live in Oxford with my family and enthusiastic, if silly, dog, Caspar.

I also love reading so that was why I jumped at the chance to retell one of my favourite novels. The author, Charles Dickens, was one of the best ever storytellers. He was born about two hundred years ago. Prepare to be scared, surprised and amused by *Great Expectations*.

Julia Golding

Part I
Chapter One

I am named after my father, Philip Pirrip, but that is an uncomfortable mouthful of pips, isn't it? You can just call me Pip. Everyone does.

I want to tell you my story, guide you through all its strange turns and twists. My tale might be a warning to some, a mystery to others. You see, before the time of my great expectations, I grew up in Kent. I lived a simple life in the countryside. Ours was the marsh country, down by the river. It is there that the first step on my adventure came on a raw afternoon towards evening. A little child, left to wander by my busy guardians, I found my way to the churchyard. In this bleak place overgrown with nettles I came across the graves of my parents. I understood then for the very first time that my father, Philip Pirrip, late of this parish, and also Georgiana, wife of the above, were dead and buried. More than this, I saw that the dark flat wilderness beyond was the marshes; the low leaden line beyond that, the river; and I was but a small bundle of shivers having to face it all on my own.

Yet while I was crying at this thought, a far more terrible realization struck. Someone else was there! A fearsome brute of a man, dressed all in grey with a clanking iron fetter on his leg, leaped out from behind a grave and swooped down on me. Soaked to the skin, scratched and bruised, he grabbed me by the chin.

'Hold your noise!' he growled. 'Keep still, you little devil, or I'll cut your throat!'

'Don't cut my throat, sir! Please don't!' I cried, shaking in my boots.

'Tell us your name! Quick!'

'Pip, sir.'

'Show us where you live.'

Too terrified to disobey, I pointed to the blacksmith's where I dwelled with my sister and her husband.

'Your mother?'

I now pointed to the grave at our feet. 'There, sir.'

'Father?'

'Him too. Late of this parish.'

'Who do ye live with – supposin' I kindly let you live, which I haven't decided yet?'

'My sister, sir – Mrs Joe Gargery – wife of the blacksmith, sir.'

The man tilted me back so that his eyes looked most powerfully down in mine. 'Blacksmith, eh? You know what a file is – for cutting through metal?'

I nodded.

'You know what wittles is?'

'That's food, isn't it, sir?'

'You get me a file.' He tilted me one way. 'And you get me wittles.' He tilted me another. 'You bring 'em both to me – or I'll have your heart and liver out.' He tilted me so I was almost upside down.

The motion made me feel as if I were aboard a ship in a storm. 'If you would kindly please keep me upright, sir, perhaps I shouldn't be sick, and perhaps I could pay more attention.'

He released me but, as I turned to go, he decided he needed a final word to hammer home his warning.

'You bring me, tomorrow morning early, that file and them wittles. You bring the lot to me at the old fort over yonder. And you never dare say a word or make a sign that you saw me. If you fail in any particular, your heart and your liver shall be tore out, roasted and ate!'

With that warning ringing in my head, I ran for home.

Chapter Two

My sister, Mrs Joe Gargery, was more than twenty years older than me. She had made herself a great reputation for generosity with the neighbours because she had brought me up after our parents' death. She never let me forget it either.

When I ran home from the churchyard, the forge was shut up early for the Christmas holiday on the next day, and Joe was sitting alone in the kitchen.

'Mrs Joe has been out a dozen times, looking for you, Pip,' said Joe. 'And she's out now, making it a baker's dozen – a whole thirteen times.'

'Is she, Joe?' I asked, coming to stand beside him.

'What's worse, she's got Tickler with her.' (Tickler was my old enemy: a piece of cane, which she often used to teach me a lesson.)

'Aye, she sat down, and she got up, and she made a grab at Tickler, and she rampaged out. That's what she did – she rampaged out.'

We could both now hear Mrs Joe approaching.

'Get behind the door, old chap,' said Joe. I hurried to obey.

My sister threw the door wide open, and finding an obstruction behind it, instantly guessed where I was hiding. She chased me over to Joe.

'Pip, you young monkey!' said Mrs Joe, stamping her foot. 'Tell me what you've been doing to wear me away with *fret* and *fright* and *worrit*, or I'll have you out of that corner though you be fifty Pips and he five hundred Gargerys!'

'I only went to the churchyard,' said I in a small voice.

'Churchyard! If it weren't for me bringing you up by hand, you'd have been in the churchyard long ago – and stayed there!' She hung up Tickler and began preparing supper. 'You'll drive me to the churchyard betwixt you, one of these days, and oh, a pr-r-recious pair you'd be without me!' Having raised the subject of my health, her thoughts turned to medicine. 'Now you come along with me and be dosed!' She grabbed me to administer her favourite medical tonic: foul-tasting tar water. I was not the only one to suffer. 'And you, don't think you'll get away without your half-pint!' she told her husband. Joe grudgingly drank his dose.

My sister replaced the bottle on the shelf, taking none herself. 'Now where was I? There's a Christmas dinner to prepare for tomorrow and a pudding to stir, from seven to eight by the clock – no slacking, mind!' She thrust the spoon at me.

As I was stirring the pudding, a gun fired in the distance. 'What's that, Joe?' I asked in a whisper.

Joe took a worried look at Mrs Joe. 'It means another convict's escaped, Pip. That's the second to run off from the prison ships since last night,' he whispered.

'Drat the boy's questions!' snapped Mrs Joe and thrust a sandwich at Joe, which was all we were to have for supper that night as she had so much to do.

Remembering the convict I met in the churchyard, I bravely persisted with my questions. 'What are prison ships, Joe?'

But Joe had received 'the look' from Mrs Joe so didn't dare speak while eating.

'Mrs Joe?' I enquired, daringly.

'Prison ships are them old boats on the river across the marshes,' Mrs Joe gestured out across the flat countryside to the river. Seeing my mouth open in wonder, she then seized her chance to stuff a sandwich in me too.

I was confused whether to eat my supper or stir the pudding, so unsuccessfully tried to do both at the same time. 'Who's put in ... ?'

My questions were too much for Mrs Joe. 'I didn't bring you up by hand to badger people's lives out. People are put in the prison ships to be transported to Australia because they murder, because they rob, and cheat, and do all sorts of bad things. But they always begin by asking questions!' She rapidly cleared the meal away before we had even finished. 'Now you get along to bed.'

I was never allowed a candle to light me to my room.
As I went upstairs in the dark, I began to worry about
the prison ships so close to my home. I was fearful that I
was clearly on my way to being put in one of them. I had
begun by *asking questions*, and I was going to rob Mrs Joe.

Since that time, which is long ago now, I have often
thought that few know how secretive young people
become when they act under terror. I was too afraid to
sleep, even if I had wanted to. As soon as the great black
velvet sky outside my little window was shot with grey, I
got up and went downstairs. Every floorboard upon the
way, and every crack, called after me, 'Stop thief!' Or,
'Get up, Mrs Joe!' I crept to the pantry to steal bread and
a pie, and filled a flask from my sister's special bottle.
I made up the level with tar water so my theft was not
immediately apparent. Next I entered the workshop to
take a file. Carrying my loot, I ran for the old fort.

But there was more than one convict abroad on the
marshes that night.

Chapter Three

The mist was heavier yet when I got out upon the marshes. I made my way to the old fort, a grassy mound right on the riverbank. Yet before I reached this landmark, I saw a man sitting on the path. His back was towards me, head nodding forward, heavy with sleep. I walked over to him softly and touched him on the shoulder. He jumped up, but it was not the convict I was looking for! Yet he was also dressed in grey, with an iron fetter on his leg. All this I saw in a moment before he swore at me and made to hit me. Terrified, I fled and left him behind in the mist.

I was soon at the old fort after that, and there was the right convict – hugging himself and limping to and fro. He was awfully cold to be sure. Relieved to find my lesser of two evils, I bundled my stolen goods into the convict's arms.

'Oh, sir. Please, take them, take them!'

The convict gave me a hungry look. 'What's in the flask, boy?'

'My sister's special cordial.'

He grinned. 'Good, is it?'

'Aye, sir. It's kept special for Uncle Pumblechook.'

'Uncle Pumblechook. Hah! I toast his health then.'

He didn't stop shivering, even after swigging the flask.

'Are you ill?' I ventured. 'The marshes – they can give people fevers.'

'I'm much of your opinion, boy, but I'll eat my breakfast before they are the death of me.' He gobbled up the food, often stopping to listen to the sounds of the river or noise of some bird. 'You brought no one with you?'

'No sir, no!' I assured him.

'I believe you. You wouldn't help hunt a poor wretched varmint.'

Pitying him as he settled down to the pie, I made bold to say, 'I am glad you enjoy it. That's my sister's meat pie, kept special … '

'For Uncle Pumblechook?'

'Aye, sir.'

Our eyes met and I thought I sensed some humour in him.

'Did you hear the cannon?' I asked, no longer so scared.

The convict shook his head.

'And did you see the other man?'

The man stopped eating and regarded me with sharp surprise. 'Where?'

'Up yonder – dressed like you.' The convict grabbed

me by the collar. 'O–only with a hat, and – and with the same reason for wanting to borrow a file.' I pointed to the convict's fetter. 'Oh and he had a badly bruised face.'

He released me. 'Not here?' He struck his own cheek with the flat of his hand.

'Yes there!'

The convict crammed the remaining food into the breast pocket of his grey jacket. 'Gentleman Compeyson – it has to be him! Give me the file! Show me the way he went, boy.'

'I don't know where he went. I couldn't see.' I gestured to the thick covering of mist.

'No matter. I'll pull him down like a bloodhound! Curse this iron on my sore leg!'

Newly afraid of the convict's fury as he hacked savagely at his chain, I fled while he was occupied.

Chapter Four

On arriving home, I fully expected to find a constable in the kitchen, waiting to arrest me. But not only was there no constable there, no discovery had yet been made of the robbery. Mrs Joe was prodigiously busy getting the house ready for Christmas dinner, and Joe had been ordered to sit on the doorstep and keep out of the way.

'And where the deuce have you been?' asked Mrs Joe.

'Been to hear the carols, sister,' I lied.

Mrs Joe attacked the floor with her broom. 'Perhaps if I weren't a blacksmith's wife, and (what's the same thing) a slave, I should have been to hear the carols. I'm rather partial to carols, myself, but do I ever get time to hear any? Hah!'

I made myself scarce. Mrs Joe was a very clean housekeeper, but had the knack of making her cleanliness more uncomfortable and unacceptable than dirt itself.

And then the time came for our Christmas dinner guests to arrive. First came Mr Pumblechook – a large hard-breathing middle-aged slow man, with a mouth like a fish. He had hair standing upright on his head, as if he had just received a terrible surprise. He was Joe's uncle but Mrs Joe had adopted him for herself.

'Mrs Joe!' cried Mr Pumblechook, ignoring Joe, his nephew. 'I have brought you, ma'am, a bottle of your favourite drink! And I have brought you, ma'am, a bottle of mine.'

Mrs Joe simpered. 'Oh, *Un-cle Pum-ble-chook*! This is kind!'

Mr Pumblechook was joined by our neighbours, Mr and Mrs Hubble, and with them the church clerk, Mr Wopsle, a man who fancied himself an actor.

'Mrs Joe!' said the clerk, throwing his arms wide and bowing.

'Mr Wopsle!' replied my sister. 'And how was the service?'

He grimaced. 'Oh dear, oh dear: the vicar! If only others were allowed to preach, such as myself, then you would have heard something worthwhile, I tell you.'

Curly-haired Mrs Hubble knew exactly how to flatter the clerk. 'But you announced the psalm most tremendously. You quite put others in the church to shame.'

He clasped his hands to his chest. 'Most kind, dear Mrs Hubble.'

Mrs Joe was not to be outdone by Mrs Hubble, her social rival. 'Would you lead us now, Mr Wopsle, in our grace?'

The clerk said a long prayer and ended with the aspiration that we might be truly grateful.

Mrs Joe poked me. 'Did you hear that? Be grateful.'

Mr Pumblechook added, 'Especially to them that brought you up.'

There were murmurs of agreement all round the table.

Mr Pumblechook returned to the earlier subject of the service, much to my relief. 'The vicar, ha! Now that was an ill-chosen sermon of his, all about peace and joy, when there are so many better subjects going about. A man needn't go far to find a subject. Look at the prodigal son!'

'True, sir,' said the clerk. 'Many a moral for the young might be deduced from that text.'

Mr Pumblechook pointed at me. 'The story tells us that the prodigal wasted his riches and ended up penniless. He was never grateful to those that brought him up.'

Joe offered me some more gravy but I was afraid to take it.

Mrs Hubble turned to my sister. 'Has the boy been a world of trouble to you, ma'am?'

'Trouble? Trouble?' my sister echoed. 'So many illnesses he's tumbled into! There were times I wished him in the churchyard but he stubbornly refused to go there!'

'More gravy, Pip, old chap?' murmured Joe again but

I was transfixed in my seat as I saw my sister bring out a familiar bottle.

'Have a little drink, Uncle,' she said, pouring him a glass.

With a sense of dread, I watched Mr Pumblechook taste, then splutter it out. 'Tar water!'

'Tar water? However could tar come there?' exclaimed Mrs Joe.

Mr Pumblechook gathered his dignity. 'Say no more on the subject. I'll have something from the bottles I brought you.' Mrs Joe served him this new beverage and we waited for his verdict. He gave an imperious nod that all was well.

Just as I thought the danger had passed, my sister rose again.

'Now, Uncle Pumblechook, you must try some of my savoury meat pie.' You may imagine my panic as she headed for the pantry. 'I set it aside especially for the occasion. Crumbly pastry. Best meat from Mr Dunstable.'

Joe misunderstood the reason for my frantic expression. 'Don't fret, Pip, you shall have some.'

Then came the scream. 'My pie!'

I ran – but got no further than the house door when I met with a sergeant and a party of soldiers. I backed away, fearing they had come to arrest me, but the officer followed me in.

'Excuse me, ladies and gentlemen,' said the sergeant, 'for interrupting your festivities. I am on the hunt in the name of the King and I need the blacksmith.'

Joe raised his hand. 'Here, sir.'

'Master Blacksmith, we've two villains to apprehend and need you to fit the manacles.'

With a nod, Joe got up and put on his coat. I began to understand that the sergeant was not there for me.

'How far would you say you were from the marshes, hereabouts? Not above a mile, I reckon?' guessed the sergeant.

'Just a mile,' confirmed Mrs Joe.

The sergeant rubbed his hands. 'That'll do. We should begin to close upon them about dusk.'

'Convicts, sergeant?' queried Mr Wopsle.

'Aye, two. They're pretty well known to be out on the marshes still, and they won't try to get clear of them before dusk. Anybody seen anything of any such game?' His eyes swept the company. Everyone hurried to deny a sighting but I studied my hands and hoped he did not ask me directly.

Joe nudged me. 'So shall we go see the hunt, Pip? You coming, Mr Wopsle?'

Mr Wopsle and I got up eagerly while the rest

suddenly looked very busy. I was eager to leave my sister and the pie far behind.

'I can't leave the ladies unprotected,' declared Mr Pumblechook.

'Couldn't possibly leave my wife at such a time,' explained Mr Hubble.

Joe lifted me onto his back. 'Right you are. We're ready, officer.'

Mrs Joe followed us to the door. 'Joe Gargery, if you bring the boy back with his head blown to bits by a musket, don't look to me to put it together again.'

No stragglers from the village joined us, for the weather was cold and threatening, the way dreary, the footing bad, darkness coming on, and the people had good fires indoors. A few faces hurried to glowing windows and looked after us, but none came out. As we made our way to the old fort, I worried for the first time whether my convict would suppose it was I who had brought the soldiers there? It was of no use asking myself this question now. There I was on Joe's back, and there was Joe beneath me, charging at the ditches like a hunter, and urging Mr Wopsle not to fall.

'There!' called a soldier. 'I see them. Convicts! Runaways!'

'Ho, Pip,' said Joe, 'they've found 'em.'

When we caught up with the soldiers, they had

surrounded the two convicts. The men were fighting each other in a ditch like wild beasts, and would have to be dragged out and separated.

'Murderer!' cried my convict.

The sergeant gestured to his men to enter the water. 'Restrain them! Surrender, confound you!'

My convict emerged from the ditch, muddy but triumphant. 'Thought you could beat me, eh? No chance.' He still held his enemy by the scruff of the neck. 'Mind, I caught him! I give him up to you.'

'Handcuffs there!' ordered the sergeant.

'Mark that!' cried the smaller man. 'Abel Magwitch tried to kill me!'

'Tried!' scoffed my convict. 'Weren't worth my while to murder him when I could do worse and drag him back! He thinks himself a gentleman, if you please, this villain. Now the ships will have their gentleman again. You used me once, Compeyson, and betrayed me at our trial – but today, I outwitted you. Could have made a dash if I hadn't found out that you was here.' He turned to the sergeant. 'I caught him. He knows it. That's enough for me.'

'Enough of this talk,' said the sergeant. 'Here, blacksmith, chain the convicts.'

Joe moved forward, leaving me to Mr Wopsle's care.

He put the irons on both convicts with his usual firm kindness.

It was then that my convict, Magwitch, saw me standing there. I shook my head and mouthed 'not me', hoping he would understand that I had not betrayed him. He frowned then turned to the sergeant and remarked, 'I wish to say something about this escape. It may prevent some persons being wrongly blamed. I took some wittles up at the village yonder.'

'You mean stole,' clarified the sergeant.

'From the blacksmith's.'

'Hah!' The sergeant looked to Joe to confirm. 'Your home?'

'So, blacksmith,' Magwitch continued. 'I'm sorry I've eaten your pie.'

The sergeant pushed the convicts to start walking. 'Get moving!'

Joe scratched his head in thought. 'You're welcome to the pie – so far as it was ever mine.'

And so we watched them go. We saw the black prison ship lying out a little way from the mud like a wrecked Noah's ark. We saw the boat go alongside, and we saw my convict taken up the side and disappear. Then, the ends of the torches were flung hissing into the water and went out, as if it were all over for him.

Chapter Five

I always knew that, when I was old enough, I was to be apprenticed to Joe. Until that time, as my sister put it, I wasn't to be 'pompeyed' – or pampered. Therefore, I was not only odd-job boy about the forge, but if any neighbour happened to want an extra boy to frighten birds, or pick up stones, or do any such job, I was told to do it. I also spent my time learning my alphabet with the help of Biddy, a young relative of Mr Wopsle. She was an orphan like me, a little neglected by her grandmother as shown by her unbrushed hair and down-at-heel shoes. Biddy and I would sit by our fire, Joe listening in and admiring, as we studied.

One night, I was sitting in the chimney corner with my slate, putting great effort into writing a note to Joe. I think it must have been a full year after our hunt upon the marshes. I read out the words I had chalked on the slate. '"Mi deer Jo. I ope u r krwite well." What do you think, Biddy?'

'Very good, Pip, but you spell 'quite' with a Q and a U, not a K and an R,' said Biddy gently.

Joe was more easily impressed. 'Astonishing, you are a scholar, Pip! Why, here's a J and an O to equal anything. And Biddy, you are quite the natural teacher! Your Uncle

Wopsle will be proud of you!'

I corrected my mistakes. 'Yes, Biddy, I couldn't have learned my letters without you.'

Biddy laughed. 'You treated the alphabet like a bramble bush, getting scratched by each and every letter.'

I chuckled at the picture. 'And now, thanks to you, I know it and can pick the fruit!'

Joe was mightily entertained by his two scholars and called to his apprentice to share in the fun. 'Listen to 'em, Orlick: we are in the presence of learning!'

Unfortunately his boy, Orlick, was of a resentful nature and replied with a murderous look.

While we were still all gathered in the kitchen, my sister came in with Mr Pumblechook.

'If this boy ain't grateful this night, he never will be,' declared Mrs Joe. 'It is only to be hoped he won't be pompeyed.'

Mr Pumblechook shook his head gravely. 'She ain't in that line, ma'am. She knows better than to pamper the boy.'

Understanding something of note had taken place concerning me, Joe dared to interrupt them. 'She?'

'Miss Havisham,' returned my sister. 'She wants this boy to go play there.' Here she began to wash my face with the corner of her apron and cluck over the state of my fingernails. 'And he had better play there or I'll teach him a lesson!'

'Miss Havisham?' repeated Joe again, bewildered.

Biddy touched his arm. 'Is that the old lady in that big house up town?'

Joe looked between me and his wife. 'How did Miss Havisham of Satis House get to know little Pip of the forge?'

'Noodle!' Mrs Joe knocked me firmly on the head even though it was Joe she was correcting. 'Uncle Pumblechook mentioned him, of course!' She turned me over to Mr Pumblechook like a jailer making a prisoner exchange.

I dragged my feet. 'But why? And what am I expected to play?'

Orlick kicked the table leg. 'He gets to play and I get to work! How is that fair?'

Mrs Joe swiped a hand at the apprentice. 'Hold your tongue, Orlick.'

Orlick glared at her. 'You don't tell me nothing, missus. I'm Joe's prentice, not yours.'

Mrs Joe put her hand to her brow. 'See what I have to endure in this house. Joe, do something!'

Joe moved to separate the two of them. 'Peace, Orlick. Mind your manners now. Pip, are you ready, little chap?'

I looked up at my oldest friend. 'Aye, Joe, but I don't know what's expected of me.'

'It's expected, boy,' announced Mr Pumblechook pompously, 'that you be ever grateful to all your friends.'

I called out my goodbyes as Mr Pumblechook marched me down the street. As we went, he barked out questions, such as 'What's seven times nine?' When given the right answer, he immediately moved on to the next: 'And four? And six?' Within a quarter of an hour we came to Miss Havisham's house, which was built of old brick, looked dismal, and had a great many iron bars on it. Mr Pumblechook knocked on the door and eventually a young lady, no older than me, answered. She was very pretty and seemed very proud.

'What name?' she asked.

'Pumblechook and Pip,' said Mr Pumblechook.

'This is Pip, is it? Come in, Pip.' She blocked the door as Mr Pumblechook made to follow. 'Oh, do you wish to see Miss Havisham?'

'If Miss Havisham wishes to see me,' replied Mr Pumblechook, his confidence dented.

'Ah, but you see, she don't,' said the girl.

Mr Pumblechook could do nothing then but eye me severely. 'Boy! Let your behaviour be a credit to them which brought you up!'

The young lady locked the gate behind us and led me into the house. On our way, we met a tall gentleman, who was just leaving.

'Mr Jaggers,' said the young lady.

He greeted her with a tip of his hat but paid little attention to me. A crowd of people, whom I later understood to be relatives of Miss Havisham, trailed after the gentleman.

'Mr Jaggers, why will Aunt Havisham not see us?' called one lady.

'That is her business, Miss Pocket,' replied Mr Jaggers.

'Yet she sees this girl ... and this boy, neither of them is her own flesh and blood.'

Her pleas had no effect. 'Quite so, madam.' Mr Jaggers tapped his hat and departed.

My guide ignored the relatives, but stopped to snatch the cap from my head and cast it on a side table. 'Go in.'

I had better manners than that. 'After you, Miss.'

She gave me a scornful glare. 'Don't be ridiculous, boy; I am not going in.'

So I entered Miss Havisham's room for the first time and stopped, astonished. I had entered a large room, well-lighted with wax candles but no daylight. Prominent in it was a draped table with a gilded looking glass. In an armchair, with an elbow resting on the table and her head leaning on that hand, sat the strangest lady I have ever seen, or shall ever see. Miss Havisham was dressed in rich materials, satins, and lace, and silks – all of white. She had a long white veil, and she had bridal flowers in her hair, but her hair was white. She had not quite finished dressing, for she had but one shoe on.

I then saw that everything within my view which ought to be white, had faded and yellowed. I saw that the bride within the bridal dress had withered like the flowers, and had no brightness left, but the brightness of her sunken eyes.

'Who is it?' asked Miss Havisham.

'Pip, ma'am.'

'Pip?'

'Mr Pumblechook's boy. Come – to play.'

'Come nearer. You are not afraid of a woman who has never seen the sun since you were born?'

'No?' I replied uncertainly.

She laid her hands over her left side. 'Do you know what I touch here?'

'Your heart?'

'Broken!' She said it with a weird smile that had a kind of boast in it. 'I am tired. I want diversion, and I have done with men and women. Play.'

I did not know where to start.

'Are you sullen and obstinate?'

'No, ma'am, I'm very sorry for you, and very sorry I can't play just now. It's so new here, and so strange, and so fine – and melancholy ... '

Miss Havisham turned back to her looking glass and began muttering. 'So new to him, so old to me; so strange to him, so familiar to me; so melancholy to the both of us. Call Estella. You can do that.'

It seemed terribly rude to roar out that young lady's name in the passageway but I had to do as I was told. 'Estella!' I called, then louder, 'Estella!'

She answered at last, and her light came along the long dark passage like a star. Miss Havisham beckoned Estella nearer and handed her a jewel.

'Your own, one day, my dear, and you will use it well.'

Estella slipped the ring on her finger. 'Thank you, I will.'

'Let me see you play cards with this boy.'

Estella sniffed disdainfully and set out the cards. 'What games do you know, boy?'

'Nothing but "beggar-my-neighbour", Miss,' I replied.

'Then beggar him, Estella,' said Miss Havisham.

We sat down to the cards and played in silence but slowly I got caught up in the game.

'My jack beats your ten!' I exclaimed, gathering my winnings.

'Your hands are coarse,' Estella declared.

I hid my hands.

'And you call knaves "jacks".'

I now felt ashamed of my ignorance. 'Your turn, Miss.'

Estella won that round. 'Your boots are too thick.'

Miss Havisham leaned towards me. 'What do you think of her?'

'I don't like to say,' I admitted.

'Tell me in my ear.'

'She is very proud ... and very pretty,' I whispered.

'Anything else?'

I felt close to tears, understanding nothing here. 'I think I should like to go home.'

'Play the game out.' Miss Havisham smiled proudly at the young lady. 'Break men's hearts, Estella, my pride and hope, break their hearts and have no mercy!'

I played the game to an end and Estella beggared me to the point where I was left with no cards.

Miss Havisham indicated that I could leave. 'Come again after six days, you hear, Pip.'

What else could I say but 'Yes, ma'am'?

'Estella, take him down and give him something to eat.'

Estella led me out, then told me to wait in the

courtyard while she fetched some food. Once she had delivered this, she left me to eat. I tried not to cry and was pleased I'd not given in as a boy of my own age entered the yard.

'Halloa![1] Young fellow!' he said. 'Who let you in?'

'Estella,' I admitted glumly.

The boy took that in his stride. 'I'm Herbert Pocket. I came with my father. Queer place, ain't it? I say, come and fight!' He held up his fists. 'Stop a minute though: I ought to give you a reason for fighting.' He butted me in the stomach. 'Laws of the game! Regular rules!' He bobbed and weaved.

I did what any boy raised in a forge would do: I levelled him with one blow.

Herbert lay on his back, waving a white handkerchief. 'That means you won.'

'Can I help you up?' I asked.

'No thankee.' He got to his feet, spirit undimmed by his defeat.

'Good afternoon.'

'Same to you,' he said cheerfully and left me.

---

[1] In Victorian times, this was an alternative spelling of the word hello, often used as an exclamation of surprise, e.g. on meeting someone unexpectedly.

Confused by this odd encounter, I turned to see Estella watching.

'You can kiss me, if you like,' she offered.

A second confusing invitation but I kissed her cheek. Laughing, she pushed me out of the gate. I scratched my head, gazing up at Satis House in utter bewilderment.

Chapter Six

I returned home to find an audience of my family and friends waiting eagerly for a report.

Joe took my cap from me and hung it on my peg. 'Pip! How was it?'

Mr Pumblechook took over the conversation before I could reply to Joe. 'Now, boy! What was Miss Havisham doing when you went in today?'

Where to start? 'Well, she ... she ... '

'I wager it was something extraordinary,' said my sister. 'She's a very fine lady, they say.'

I feared I would not be believed if I told the truth so instead my brain started spinning a most fantastical description. 'She was ... she was sitting in a black velvet coach.'

'A black velvet coach?' repeated Mr Pumblechook and Mrs Joe.

'Yes. And Miss Estella – her niece, I think – handed her cake and a crystal glass on a gold plate.'

'Where was this coach?' asked Mrs Joe, brow furrowed.

I was perfectly frantic – a reckless witness under torture. 'In Miss Havisham's room – but there weren't any horses to it.'

'Can this be possible, Uncle?' marvelled my sister.

'I'll tell you, ma'am, my opinion is that it's a sedan chair,' said Mr Pumblechook. 'She's flighty – quite flighty enough to pass her days in a sedan chair. What did you play at, boy?'

'We played ... with flags.' Imaginary flags popped up in my brain.

'Flags!' exclaimed Biddy, looking at me suspiciously.

'Excellent!' declared Mr Wopsle.

I'd gone too far to back down now. 'Yes, Estella waved a blue and I a red and Miss Havisham one all sprinkled over with little gold stars. And we all waved swords and hurrahed!'

'Well I never!' said Mrs Joe. 'Where did you get the swords from?'

'Out of a cupboard. And I saw pistols in it – and jam – and pills.'

Mr Pumblechook nodded gravely. 'That's true, ma'am, for that much I've seen myself.'

I looked at him in surprise.

Mrs Joe folded her arms. 'Gracious.'

Mr Pumblechook loomed over me. 'Does she want you back, boy?'

'Yes, sir.'

'See,' he appealed to the company, 'I was right: she means to do something for him.' Mr Pumblechook rising was the signal for everyone to leave. My sister hurried out after him, brimming over with excitement.

That left Joe and me alone in the kitchen.

I hung my head. 'Joe, I have something to tell you.'

'Yes, Pip?'

'All that about Miss Havisham? All lies.'

Joe thought about this a moment. 'Even the flags?'

I nodded.

'Pip, old chap, what possessed you?'

The memory of the humiliating visit washed over me. 'I don't know, but I wish my boots weren't so thick, nor my hands so coarse. And I wish I'd learned to call jacks "knaves."'

Joe sighed. 'There's one thing you may be sure of, Pip: lies is lies. Don't you tell me no more of 'em, Pip.'

I hated more than anything to disappoint him. 'You're not angry with me, Joe?'

'No, old chap.' Joe held out his hand and I shook it.

That was a memorable day, for it made great changes in me. But it is the same with any life. Imagine one selected day struck out of your life, and think how different its course would have been.

Chapter Seven

I continued my visits to Miss Havisham over the next few years. My sister and Mr Pumblechook never ceased to speculate as to what the lady might do for me. Joe remained silent during these discussions, working at the anvil with the grudging aid of Orlick, now promoted to journeyman, a qualified blacksmith. A strange, jealous person, Orlick made no secret of the fact that he would like nothing better than to see me come to nothing. Orlick's desire to be treated better than he deserved led to furious arguments with my sister, who was quick to silence anyone who challenged her rule. Sharp words were exchanged and objects broken and only Joe's intervention stopped their rows spiralling into worse violence.

I deeply disliked Orlick but I spent little time thinking about the problems at the forge – I was too busy thinking about myself. I did not know what to make of my position. Was I Miss Havisham's protégé, destined to marry her beautiful foster child, Estella; or was I merely an amusement whom she would return to Joe and the smithy when she was done with me? Just in case, I worked hard on educating myself to prepare for life at Estella's side, aided by my first teacher, Biddy. With her gentle

help, I soon outstripped Biddy in learning and begun
to think very highly of myself, ashamed though I am to
admit it now.

Then one day, as Miss Havisham and I were walking
in her garden, she stopped short and said, with some
displeasure, 'You are growing tall, Pip! Taller than me!'
She said no more but the thought lodged in her mind and
the following day she told me to bring Joe to see her.

So that was how Joe came to be standing in her
presence, decked out in his Sunday clothes, making
himself dreadfully uncomfortable entirely on my account.
Miss Havisham was seated at her dressing table but
looked round as Estella ushered us in.

'You are the husband of the sister of this boy?' Miss
Havisham asked.

Joe's nerves got the better of him so he addressed his
answer to me. 'Tell 'er "Yes", Pip.'

'And you reared the boy with the intention of making
him your apprentice, is that so, Mr Gargery?'

'You know, Pip, that you and me were ever friends
and it were looked forward to betwixt us.' Joe gained a
little confidence remembering our plans made by the
kitchen fire.

'You expected no reward for lending me the boy?'
I nudged my friend, whose hurt at such a suggestion

had robbed him of speech. 'Joe!'

'But that ain't no question requiring an answer betwixt us and which you know to be full well *No*!' he replied.

Miss Havisham gave one of her smiles that suggested she knew Joe better than he did himself. She held out a bag of coins. 'Pip has earned a reward here. Five-and-twenty guineas to buy an apprenticeship with you. Give it to your master, Pip. Goodbye, Pip. Let them out, Estella.'

It was a shock to be thus cast out. 'Am I to come again, Miss Havisham?' I asked.

Miss Havisham was losing interest, already turning back to her glass. 'No. Gargery is your master now.'

'But Miss Havisham!'

'I suppose you may come on your birthday,' she replied languidly.

After Estella had locked the gate behind us with no sign she regretted my departure, both Joe and I stopped outside the forbidding front of Satis House.

'Astonishing!' said Joe.

His honest confusion tickled my humour. 'Astonishing,' I echoed. It was like a spell had broken and we both laughed, setting off for home in a cheerful frame of mind. On the way, however, we met Orlick skulking about the road.

'Halloa, Orlick! What are you doin' 'ere?' called Joe, surprised to see his journeyman away from the forge.

Orlick pointed at me. 'He's not the only one can take half a day off.' He fell into step with us as a gun boomed across the marsh. 'Guns is going again. Some of them birds flown the cage.' He began humming a tune Joe often sang while hammering at the anvil, keeping time with his fists.

As we approached the forge, Biddy came running down the road towards us, her face pale with horror. 'Quick, Joe! There's something wrong up at your place. Run!'

'Hah! What's this?' Joe set off at a sprint for home.

I grabbed her elbow. 'What's happened, Biddy?'

She clung to me. 'Someone's attacked Mrs Joe – in her own house and all!'

I rushed home and found Joe cradling my sister in his arms. She had been beaten senseless and it was clear that the tool used to hit her was my convict's rusty fetter. Someone must have found it at the old fort. Guilt hit me when I recalled that I had provided the file with which the convict had cut the chain.

Orlick tugged the manacles from my cold fingers and waggled the chain with a sneer. 'Oh, what a shame. But there's many as wanted her silenced.' He gave me a look as if to say he knew that my secret desire had been accomplished.

'No, I never ... not that ... not like this,' I stuttered.

'No more rampaging from 'er, eh?' Orlick dumped the manacles and went out whistling.

Though Biddy and I suspected that Orlick had attacked my sister, we had no proof. When she awoke, Mrs Joe was so different, so childlike, that she could not tell us who had hit her. Instead she followed Orlick around, ever anxious to keep him happy. He did not know what to make of this behaviour, any more than I did.

Chapter Eight

For the next few years, I fell into a regular routine working as Joe's apprentice in the forge. The only breaks to that pattern were my birthday visits to Miss Havisham, made partly in the hope of seeing Estella. Meanwhile, Biddy became the centre of our household, nursing Mrs Joe and taking over the tasks my sister used to do. I worked long hours, then spent every evening studying.

'Biddy,' I asked one day, 'how do you manage it? Either I am very stupid or you are very clever.'

'What is it I manage?' Biddy asked, putting the kettle over *the* fire.

'Since *you*'ve moved in after ... well, you know,' I nodded my *head* to my poor sister in her chair by the *hearth*, 'you manage the house and keep up with my *studies*.'

She smiled. 'I suppose I *must* catch it – like a cough.'

I turned a *page* but I wasn't *really* thinking of my notes. 'You are one *of* those, Biddy, *who* make the most of every change. You never had the chance before you came here, and see how improved you are.'

Biddy smoothed her apron, *her voice* a little choked. 'I was your first teacher though, wasn't *I*?'

'Biddy, why are you crying?'

She shook her head vigorously. 'No, I'm not. Whatever gave you that idea?' She turned back to supper preparations.

My golden prospects, so often discussed by others in front of that same fire, danced before me in the flames like tempting dreams. 'Biddy, I want to be a gentleman.'

Biddy stood up sharply. 'Oh, I wouldn't if I was you!'

'But I have a particular reason.'

'You know best, Pip; but don't you think you're happier as you are?'

'Biddy, I'm not at all happy as I am. If only I could have settled down and been half as fond of the forge as I was when I was little, I know it would have been much better for me. Joe and I would perhaps have become partners, and I might even have grown up to marry you. I should have been good enough for you, shouldn't I, Biddy?'

Biddy sighed. 'Yes, I'm not over-particular.'

'Instead I was told I was coarse and common and now I'm dissatisfied and uncomfortable.' The insult still burned hot in my soul.

'Who told you that?' Biddy asked indignantly.

'The beautiful lady at Miss Havisham's. Estella.'

Biddy's frown deepened. 'So do you want to be a

gentleman to spite her or gain her affection? If it is to spite her, then it is better to care nothing for her words. If it is to impress her, I should think – but you know best – she's not worth it if she doesn't love you as you are.'

It was so hopeless – I was an apprentice blacksmith, not a gentleman. 'I don't know, Biddy, but I do admire her dreadfully.'

The bell above our door rang and Biddy went to answer. Joe came in from the forge, wiping his brow. Biddy returned with a stranger, a man I remembered from my very first visit to Miss Havisham. This gentleman had deep-set eyes and black bushy eyebrows.

'I have reason to believe there is a blacksmith here, by the name Joseph, or Joe, Gargery,' announced the man.

'Aye, sir.' Joe put aside the towel on which he had been wiping his hands.

'You have an apprentice, commonly known as Pip?'

'Here, sir!' I rose from my seat.

The man came to stand in the centre of the room, in command as in a courtroom. 'My name is Jaggers, a lawyer in London. I come here on behalf of an anonymous client. Now Joseph Gargery, I am the bearer of an offer to relieve you of this young fellow, your apprentice. You would not object to releasing him from his apprenticeship? You would not want money for so doing?'

'No!' exclaimed Joe, with a glance at me.

Mr Jaggers held up a finger. 'Very well. Remember what you have just said. Now I return to this young fellow. The news I bring is that he is to inherit a handsome sum of money. He is to be removed from his present sphere of life and be brought up as a gentleman – in a word, he is a young fellow of great expectations!'

My mind immediately leaped to the conclusion that it was Miss Havisham behind this extraordinary offer.

'Now, Mr Pip, there are two conditions. First, my client instructs that you always bear the name of Pip. Secondly, Mr Pip, the name of your patron is to remain a profound secret, until that person chooses to reveal it. Do you object?'

'I have no ... no objections.'

Jaggers gave me a hard stare. 'I should think not! There is already a sum of money in my hands to pay for your education and maintenance. Please consider me your guardian. Well, Joseph Gargery? You look dumbfounded.'

Joe was shaking his head. 'I am!'

'What if I told you that my client instructed me to make you a present to compensate you for the loss of Mr Pip's services?'

Joe's indignation flared. 'Pip is hearty welcome to go

free to honour and fortune. But if you think as money can compensate me for the loss of the little child – he that came to the forge – and was ever the best of friends ... !' Biddy went to Joe's side to comfort him.

Mr Jaggers cast a dubious look at Joe. 'Mr Pip, I think the sooner you leave the better!' With that parting thought, he left us.

From his seat on a low stool, Joe cupped his knees with his big hands and looked up at me. 'Well now, our Pip, a gentleman of fortun' and Lord bless him in it!' There was a certain touch of sadness to his congratulations that I resented.

Dizzied by my new prospects, I promised myself that I would do something for the poor people of the village. I planned to give them at the very least a dinner of roast beef and plum pudding. I had a new suit made for my London life, much to the delight of the local tailor. At home, I thought myself so fine that I pompously handed out words of unnecessary advice to those I loved best.

'While I am away, you will take every opportunity to help Joe on a little?' I urged Biddy. 'Improving his learning and manners and so on?'

Biddy bristled. 'Oh, his manners! Won't his manners do then?'

I gestured around our humble kitchen as if that spoke

for itself. 'My dear Biddy, they do very well here but ... '

Biddy slammed the frying pan onto the stove. 'Have you never considered that he may be proud? And rightly so, as he is kind, and competent, and the people respect him as he is.'

'Now, Biddy, I'm sorry to see you like this – it's as if you envy and begrudge me my rise in fortune.'

She stood up proudly. 'Whether you scold me or not, you may depend on me to try to do all that I can to help here.'

Our neighbours were pleased to hear of my good fortune, most of all Mr Pumblechook. On hearing the news, he came to visit, pumping my hand up and down as if he was in expectation of my mouth gushing money.

'My dear friend, I wish you joy in your good fortune,' he said. 'Ah, it is sad to reflect that she who brought you up is no longer able to understand the honour that has been done to you!'

Indeed, my sister had shown no sign she understood even though Biddy had patiently tried to explain.

'To think that I should have been the humble cause of your great good fortune!' continued Mr Pumblechook with great self-satisfaction.

Before I left for London, I wanted to at least make one attempt to thank my patron, so I called on Satis House even though it wasn't time for one of my birthday visits. I found Miss Havisham as usual amidst her dusty bridal feast, but this time she was in the care of Miss Pocket, one of the poor relations.

'You! Good gracious! What do you want?' asked Miss Havisham.

I bowed low. 'I'm about to leave for London, Miss Havisham, and I wanted to say goodbye.'

She waved her walking stick at my new suit as a fairy godmother does a wand. 'You look very smart, Pip.'

I felt sure she understood I meant to thank her as my secret benefactor but neither of us could speak openly. 'I have come into such good fortune since I last saw you – and I am grateful for it, Miss Havisham.'

'I have seen Mr Jaggers and have heard about it, Pip. So you go tomorrow?'

'Yes, Miss Havisham. And may I bid Miss Estella farewell?'

Miss Havisham gave one of her unsettling, triumphant smiles. 'She's gone abroad to finish her education. She is now far out of your reach, prettier than ever, admired by all who see her. Do you feel you have lost her?'

I did not know what to reply to that.

Miss Havisham held out her wrinkled hand.

'Be good, deserve your fortune, listen to Mr Jaggers's instructions. Goodbye.'

I kneeled and kissed her hand.

And so I left my fairy godmother standing in the midst of the dimly lit drawing room beside the rotten wedding cake that was hidden in cobwebs.

There was now nothing left to do but bid farewell to all from my village. Joe and Biddy were the hardest to leave.

'Remember, such larks, Pip!' said Joe, squeezing me to his chest.

Things had remained cool between Biddy and me since our argument. 'Biddy?'

At this final moment, Biddy forgave me. 'Look after yourself, Pip!' She wiped away tears with her apron.

Returning Joe's wave, I whistled and pretended I was happy to leave, until by the fingerpost at the end of the village I broke into tears. I was better for it – more sorry, more aware of my own ingratitude, more gentle. But the mists had all lifted now and the world lay spread before me. I was off to London!

Part II
Chapter One

Now is the time to tell you how my great expectations proceeded in London. My first act was to seek out Mr Jaggers, whom I found in his office in the shadow of Newgate Prison, final destination of criminals and those in debt. He arrived accompanied by his clerk and followed by a crowd of clients, all crying out for his attention.

Mr Jaggers dismissed the first man who stood in his path. 'Now I have nothing to say to you. The result of your case, it's a toss-up. Have you paid Wemmick?'

'Yes, sir, but … ' the man replied.

Jaggers held up his finger. 'I won't have it. If you say a word, I'll give up the case.'

Another desperate man scrunched up his cap and bowed before him. 'Sir, Mr Jaggers, sir! My brother–'

Mr Jaggers waved him aside. 'Too late, I am on the other side.' The man retreated, broken-hearted. 'Ah, Mr Pip.'

I stood up, trying not to look like yet another supplicant.

Mr Jaggers beckoned me to follow him into his private office.

'You are on time, I see.' He began eating his lunch, having no minute to spare in his busy day.

'Here's your allowance.' The clerk handed over a purse. 'You'll find your credit good, but I shall check your bills and warn you if you are in danger of getting too far into debt. Of course you'll go wrong somehow, but that's no fault of mine. You are to lodge with Mr Herbert Pocket. Wemmick will make the introductions. You'll room in Barnard's Inn. Now off you go.'

That was all the lecture my London guardian gave me before sending me back out onto the street. Wemmick took me to my lodgings and left me in the care of a pale young gentleman of about my own age.

'Mr Pip?' asked the gentleman.

'Mr Pocket?'

Then he grinned. 'Lord bless me, you're Miss Havisham's boy?'

The memory rushed back. 'And you're the fighting young gentleman!'

'Indeed I am.' He gestured me to take a seat. 'I heard you have come into your good fortune very recently. I was rather on the lookout for one when I met you.'

'Indeed?'

'Yes. Miss Havisham sent for me. My father's one of her cousins but he refuses to flatter her like the rest of her relations. I went to Satis House to see if she would like me. Clearly, she didn't. Make yourself at home.'

He offered me one of the strawberries he had recently purchased.

'Thank you.'

He popped one in his own mouth. 'Ah yes, if she had liked me, I was to be what-you-call-it to Estella.'

'What's that?'

'Engaged.'

'How can you bear your disappointment?'

Herbert laughed at my serious tone. 'Hah! I didn't care much for it. She's frightening.'

'Miss Havisham?'

'I meant Estella. The girl's hard, haughty and capricious – brought up to take revenge on the male sex.'

With Herbert as my guide, I was soon familiar with the pleasures of London. He introduced me to his friends and we settled in to live extremely well, spending more than we had in the bank. I met two of Herbert's best friends, Drummle and Startop, at the first card party at our lodgings.

Startop greeted me with genuine warmth. 'Mr Pip – delighted to meet you.'

'And I you, sir.'

Drummle, however, was an unpleasant fellow who made no secret that he despised us. 'Charmed I'm sure. Get on and deal the cards, man.'

Herbert didn't seem to mind his rudeness, too good-humoured to let others bother him. 'Pip and I first met at the house of a queer old relative of mine. A Miss Havisham. Lives in seclusion but is worth a pretty penny,' he explained.

Startop looked at his hand and grimaced. 'Nothing better than rich relatives. They have a habit of dying and leaving one money.'

'Not this one. I won't see a farthing. She's taken against the entire male race, with one possible exception.' Herbert nodded at me.

'How did she get to be as she is; do you know?' I asked.

Herbert laid down a heart. 'Oh yes. I heard it from my father. Her brother held a deep grudge against her, and schemed to get his hands on her share of the family fortune.'

'Her own brother?'

'Half-brother in truth. He introduced her to a fraudster, not a true gentleman, but Miss Havisham was persuaded to fall in love with him.'

Drummle snorted and placed his card on top of Herbert's.

'This fraudster got great sums from her, which he divided with her brother. The marriage day was fixed, the wedding dresses bought, the honeymoon planned, the guests invited. The day came, but not the bridegroom.'

Drummle scooped up the cards. 'Saw that one coming a mile off.'

Herbert nodded an acknowledgement. 'He wrote her a letter, which she received while dressing for her wedding at twenty minutes to nine. At which she stopped all the clocks, laid the whole place waste, and has never since looked upon the light of day.'

Chapter Two

While the mystery of Miss Havisham was now explained, the puzzle of how to make ends meet as a gentleman was not. Bills poured in but I had spent all my money, which meant I had to make another visit to Mr Jaggers. He showed no surprise that I had already run out of cash and sent me to see his clerk.

'Mr Wemmick, Mr Jaggers sent me to you. To ask for twenty pounds, sir,' I said.

Wemmick looked up from his high desk. 'Twenty pounds already, is it? Let me see.' He counted out the money. 'And what do you make of Mr Jaggers, Mr Pip?'

'I don't know.'

'Excellent. He'll take it as a compliment. Always seems to me he is like a hidden trap. Suddenly – *click* – you're caught!' He handed me the money. 'It don't signify to you with your brilliant lookout, but as to myself, my guiding star always is "Get hold of portable property". Will you take supper with me? In Walworth?'

'Gladly.'

Wemmick put on his coat and led the way out of the office, heading for home. 'You won't object to meeting my aged parent, I hope?'

'Of course not.'

'Have you visited Mr Jaggers at home yet?' Wemmick's quick changes of subject kept surprising me – indeed, he really was a most intriguing man.

'Not yet.'

'He'll give you a good dinner.'

'I look forward to it.'

'Mr Jaggers is to ask you and your pals, Mr Pocket, Mr Startop and Mr Drummle to dinner.'

'I'm not sure I'd count Mr Drummle as a pal.'

'He intends to invite the whole gang. When you are there, make sure you take a close look at his housekeeper.'

'Shall I see anything strange?'

'You'll see a wild one tamed, thanks to Mr Jaggers's skill. Keep your eye on her.'

We had left the city far behind and arrived at a quaint gothic house very much like a castle, complete with guns, flagpole and drawbridge.

Wemmick stopped before it, his pride clear. 'My own doing. Looks pretty, don't it? At nine o'clock every night, Greenwich time, the gun fires. And after I have crossed the bridge, I hoist it up – so – and cut off communication. It brushes the Newgate cobwebs away.'

Once inside, Wemmick introduced me to those waiting for him in the kitchen. 'My aged parent and our neighbour, Miss Skiffins.' He bent closer to his father and shouted. 'Well, Aged Parent, how are you?'

'All right, John, all right,' the old man bellowed.

'Here's Mr Pip, Aged Parent, and I wish you could hear his name.' Taking a seat beside the prim Miss Skiffins, his sweetheart, Wemmick put his arm around her. 'You talk to him, Mr Pip.'

'This is a fine place of my son's, sir!' thundered the old man.

'It is indeed,' I agreed. 'I hope Mr Jaggers admires it?'

Wemmick flinched. 'Never seen it. Never heard of it. Never seen the aged. When I go into the office, I leave the castle behind me, and when I come into the castle, I leave the office behind me. If you would not mind, I'd be grateful if you did the same.' He checked his pocket watch and jumped up. 'Ah, getting near gunfire, Miss Skiffins. It's the aged parent's treat, Mr Pip, as it's the only thing he can hear clearly. He'll be eighty-two next birthday. I have a notion of firing eighty-two times, if the neighbourhood shouldn't complain.'

With Miss Skiffins's blessing, Wemmick rushed out and fired the gun. The aged parent nodded and clapped. Then followed a delightful supper and an overnight stay for me in a turret bedroom. It wasn't until the next morning as we returned to Newgate that

Wemmick changed. With every step, he got drier and harder, his mouth firming into a postbox slit. By the time we reached his office, Walworth and the aged parent were as distant as Newgate had been from us last night.

Chapter Three

Settled in my new life in London, I rarely spared a thought for those I had left behind at the forge. Someone from that life, however, came to me. Estella returned to England and Miss Havisham wrote to request that I escort Estella to her new home. Having never forgotten the proud girl from Satis House, it was with great excitement that I rushed to the inn to meet Estella. She was waiting with a maid beside a great pile of luggage.

'You got my note?' Estella asked.

'Yes, yes indeed, Estella. It has been so long!' The years had been kind to her: she had grown in beauty. Once again, she made me feel nothing but a common boy in contrast.

Estella looked at me with her usual disdain. 'Miss Havisham says you are to escort me to Richmond. This is my purse, and you are to pay my expenses out of it.' I made a move to refuse it. 'Oh, you must take my purse! We are not free to follow our own rules, you and I. We have to do what others want.'

I offered my arm but she straightened her gloves instead. 'What will you do at Richmond?' I asked.

'I am going to live, at great expense, with a lady there, who will introduce me into the best society.'

'I suppose you will be glad of variety and admiration?'

'Yes, I suppose so.' Her lack of enthusiasm was striking.

Just as I had when we were children, I found her manner very confusing. 'You speak of yourself as if you were someone else.'

'Come, come.' Estella smiled at me as if she found me amusing. 'You must not expect me to take a lesson from you. I must talk in my own way. How do you find living with Mr Pocket?'

'As pleasant as I could live anywhere, away from you.' I felt as if I was losing my chance with her.

'You silly boy, how can you talk such nonsense?'

I helped her into the carriage. 'Do you remember how you made me cry the first time we met?'

'Did I? No, I don't remember.' Her gaze was vacant as she looked out the window. 'You must know that I have no heart – if that has anything to do with my memory.'

It was such a bleak announcement that I had to protest. 'I must doubt that. There can be no beauty without it.'

'Oh! I have a heart to be stabbed or shot; and of course, if it ceased to beat I should cease to be. But you know what I mean. I have no softness there, no – sympathy – feeling – none of that nonsense.' She seemed puzzled by her own confession.

'Surely ... ?'

'I am serious. If we are to spend much time together, you had better believe it at once.' She raised a hand to pre-empt the question I was about to ask. 'And no, I have not given my love to anyone else. I have never had any such thing to give.'

The carriage turned out of the inn yard.

Estella gave me a brittle smile. 'Come! You shall not shed tears for my cruelty today; you shall be my page and give me your service until Richmond.'

I took her hand and raised it to my lips. 'I wonder Miss Havisham has not requested that you return home to her.'

'It is all part of her plans for me, Pip.' Taking back her hand, Estella sighed as if she were tired. 'I am to write to her constantly and tell her how I get on.'

It was the first time she had ever called me by name. Of course she did so on purpose, knowing I should treasure the memory.

Chapter Four

As Wemmick had hinted, my three card-playing friends and I received an invitation to dine at Mr Jaggers's. His was a rather stately sort of house in Soho but dolefully in want of painting and the windows dirty.

Mr Jaggers came out to greet us. 'Gentlemen, welcome. Mr Pip, Mr Pocket, and this is?'

'Mr Startop, sir,' I said.

Startop walked forward holding out his hand but Jaggers swept by on a course for Drummle.

'Not him, I mean the other. I like the look of that fellow.' Mr Jaggers was sizing Drummle up as a future customer; he shook his hand enthusiastically.

'Bentley Drummle, sir.' Drummle gave the lawyer a curt nod.

Mr Jaggers ushered us into his dining room and moved to the drinks tray.

'A spider, that's what your friend is,' the lawyer said aside to me, meaning Drummle. 'Used to lying in wait with all the patience of that creature. Added to that, he has a foolish confidence in his money and in his family's greatness. He'll watch, uncoil and drop down on his prey in the nick of time.'

Turning back to the company, Mr Jaggers offered each

a glass from a fine crystal decanter. 'Help yourself to a drink before dinner. Mr Drummle, sit by me if you please.' As we took our places, the housekeeper entered with our food. I watched her closely for signs of her wildness as Wemmick had advised: she was tall and pale, with a mass of streaming hair. Her face held a curious fluttering expression, lips parted as if breathless.

Mr Jaggers appeared to pay her no attention. 'So, how do you like these fellows, Drummle?'

'I prefer their absence to their company, but I can beat 'em, hands down, at rowing.' Drummle flexed his arms, showing off muscle. His effect on the housekeeper was marked. She stopped in her duties and stared at him, transfixed, squeezing her cloth between her hands.

'How interesting.' Mr Jaggers reached out and grabbed his housekeeper's arm. 'But if you talk of strength, I'll show you a wrist.'

The housekeeper drew back. 'Master, don't.'

'There's power here – force of grip, enough to kill a man, or woman.' With a warning look, he released her. 'That'll do, Molly. You've been admired, now you can go.'

After that alarming meal, we left Mr Jaggers and went to a tavern to continue the evening. We fell to proposing toasts to the ladies that we admired, or fancied ourselves in love with, until Drummle made one that I could not let pass.

'I'll give you a lady,' cried Drummle. 'A toast. To Estella!'

'Estella?' I asked. The name was not common.

'Estella of Richmond,' Drummle leered at me.

I stood up. 'You ... you know no such lady! It is disrespectful of you to even mention her name. And ... and if you continue to do so, I will challenge you to a duel!'

My rash words were met with silence.

'Pip,' implored Herbert.

'Your proof you know her, sir?' I persisted.

Drummle swallowed his drink slowly, taunting me. 'I had the honour of dancing with her. Several times.'

His sneering expression made me realize I had made a fool of myself. 'Well, in that case, I regret I spoke so hastily.' I sat down. 'I beg your pardon. I am not challenging you to anything.'

Drummle grinned at me. 'Of course, you aren't.'

'It was only a toast, Pip,' whispered Herbert.

Only when I was alone again with my room-mate, was I able to give vent to my feelings.

'O Herbert, whatever is she doing with that foul

spider of a man? What can she see in him?'

Herbert gave me a wry look. 'No idea, Pip. Do you think it could be his looks, fortune, family and social connections perhaps?'

I clutched my heart. 'What is that weighed against love? I love – I adore Estella.' There: I had made my confession!

'Well?' said Herbert.

'Well, Herbert? Is that all you have to say? Well?'

'What next, I mean? Of course, I know that you adore her.'

'How? I never told you.'

'Told me! You have never told me when you have got your hair cut, but I have had eyes to see it. You adore Estella – always have. As for me, I adore Clara.'

'The young lady you have been courting?' I'd suspected Herbert had a sweetheart but so far he had not introduced us.

'The very one. Miss Clara Barley.'

'So that's her name. When am I to meet her?'

'Soon I hope, Pip. But I have to confess that my mother thinks she isn't good enough to marry into our family. Her father has a business furnishing ships on the Thames – in trade, you know? So ... ' He shrugged.

'Without your family's blessing, you can't afford

to marry her while you are still trying to establish yourself in the world.' I threw an arm around Herbert's shoulders. 'What a sorry pair we are, Herbert.'

'And dreadfully in debt. You know, Pip: I think I'll buy myself a rifle, go to America and hunt buffaloes to make my fortune.'

Chapter Five

One day soon after, a letter came, telling me that my sister, Mrs Joe, had died. I returned home for the funeral only to find Mr Pumblechook had taken control of the ceremony.

'Dear Joe, how are you?' I asked my oldest friend as the black-plumed procession left the house.

Joe stood by in bewilderment as his wife's funeral was taken out of his hands by a man who had shown little interest in my sister since her accident. 'Pip, old chap, you knowed her when she were a fine figure of a—'

'Pocket handkerchiefs out, all!' ordered Mr Pumblechook, enjoying his role of chief mourner.

Joe dabbed his eyes. 'I meantersay, Pip, I would have preferred to carry her to the church myself, but it were considered that the neighbours would look down on such.' In other words, Mr Pumblechook had trampled over Joe's genuine grief. Poor Joe!

After the service, I found Biddy among the neighbours come to say their farewells. Without my sister in the house, Biddy could no longer stay, as a single woman could not live alone with an unmarried man.

'How are you going to live now, Biddy?' I asked. 'If you want any money—'

She stopped me before I went any further. 'I am going to try to get the place of the mistress in the new school. You know, Mr Pip, the new schools are not like the old, but I learned a good deal with you, and have had time since then to improve.'

'I think you would always improve, Biddy, under any circumstances. I shall be down often now. I'm not going to leave poor Joe alone.' Biddy folded her arms. 'Don't you believe me?'

'Yes, Mr Pip.'

'Why are you calling me Mr Pip, Biddy, when I've always been plain Pip to you – what do you mean?'

'What do I mean?'

'Now don't echo. You never used to echo, Biddy.'

'Never used! O Mr Pip! *Used!*'

'Biddy, I made a remark about my coming down here often, to see Joe, but you are acting as if you don't believe me. Have the goodness, Biddy, to tell me why.'

'Are you quite sure, then, that you *will* come to see him often?'

'Oh dear me! You are showing a very bad side of human nature to doubt me so!' I scolded her.

Joe found us among the mourners and took Biddy's arm.

'I'll be off now, Joe,' I said.

'All right, Pip.' Joe wiped his hand to shake mine.

'No, don't wipe it off – for heaven's sake, give me your hand just as it is! I shall be down soon, and often.' I gave Biddy a pointed look.

'Never too soon, sir, and never too often, Pip,' said Joe.

I lowered my voice as I took Biddy's hand. 'Biddy, I'm not angry, but I am hurt.'

Biddy bit her lip. 'No, don't be hurt. Let me be the one hurt, if I have been unfair.'

Good intentions rarely last, as Biddy knew better than I. Such thoughts of regular visits to those I left behind were driven out by my turning twenty-one. I came of age and into five hundred pounds per year. Though I'm pleased to say that I did one thing of which I can still be proud. After receiving the money, I sought out Mr Jaggers's clerk.

'Mr Wemmick, I want to help a friend. Mr Pocket. He needs but a little money to set him up in business and I count myself fortunate to be able to give him some.'

Wemmick glared at me over the top of his desk. 'Choose your bridge, Mr Pip, and pitch your money into the Thames – you might as well throw it away than give it to a friend. It amounts to the same thing.'

'This is your final word, Mr Wemmick?'

'My final word – *in this office.*' His tone made me pause.

'Ah, but what would be your word in Walworth?'

Wemmick closed his ledger with a bang. 'Mr Pip, Walworth is one place, and this office is another. Much as the aged parent is one person, and Mr Jaggers is another. They must not be muddled up.'

'Then might I come home with you?'

'With pleasure, Mr Pip.'

Once we were away from Newgate, I repeated my question.

Wemmick was now smiling and eager to help. 'In this case, Mr Pip, I might use your money to get Mr Pocket a job with a relative of Miss Skiffins – one Mr Clarriker, a merchant of good reputation. And I can do it so your Mr Pocket never suspects who has helped him!'

'That is just what is needed. Thank you, Mr Wemmick.' We left each other much satisfied that Mr Pocket would be a step nearer to happiness with his Clara.

Chapter Six

I returned home in wretched weather: stormy and wet, and mud, mud, mud, deep in all the streets. So furious had been the gusts, that high buildings in town had had the lead stripped off their roofs; and in the country, trees had been torn up, and sails of windmills carried away; and gloomy accounts had come in from the coast, of shipwreck and death.

I found a man waiting for me on the stairs to my rooms – a strong, muscular figure aged about sixty, salt-stained and roughly dressed, like a voyager just arrived in port.

'Excuse me, but what is your business here?' I asked.

'I wish to come in, Mister.'

Not knowing how to refuse him, I cautiously let him in, but took hold of a candlestick to defend myself. The man made no threatening moves but looked about admiringly, as if he were responsible for what he saw.

'You will explain yourself now?' I asked, wishing to get this interview swiftly over.

The man held out his hand but I kept my distance. He lowered it with a sigh.

'It's disappointin' to a man after having looked for'ard so long, and come so far; but you're not to blame for that. There's no one here, is there?'

'Why do you ask me that?'

'You're a game one. I'm glad you've grow'd up a game one!' He moved swiftly, grabbing my hand and kissing my knuckles. 'You acted noble once, my boy – and I have never forgot it! Noble Pip!'

The realization hit me that I was facing my convict. I pulled away. 'Stay back! If you've come here to thank me for what I did as a little child, it's really not necessary! Look, you're wet and weary. Will you drink something before you go?' I would do everything quickly so I could hurry him out of the door.

Magwitch, as I remembered him to be called, still watched me. 'Aye, I will drink afore I go.'

I felt a little ashamed of my reaction to him. My visitor had offered me no violence. 'I hope that you'll not think I spoke harshly to you just now. I'm sorry for it if I did. I wish you well and happy. How are you?'

Magwitch took the drink I offered. 'I've been a sheep farmer, stockbreeder, other trades besides, away in the New World, many a thousand mile of stormy water from England. I've done wonderful well.'

'I'm glad to hear it.'

'I hoped to hear you say so, my dear boy. I'm famous for it. Abel Magwitch – sheep baron.' He took a seat on one side of the fire. 'May I be so bold as ask you how you have done, since you and me was out on them lone shivering marshes?'

'How I've done?' I sat opposite him.

'Aye.' Magwitch's eyes glinted with cunning.

'I ... I was chosen to inherit some money.'

'Might a mere varmint ask whose money?' He tapped his glass.

'I don't know.' But his expression was making me doubt everything I thought I knew.

'But the money was controlled by a guardian while you was under age. Some lawyer, first letter beginning with J?' Magwitch knew too much and was looking at me as if he owned everything he saw. He said he had become a rich man. It couldn't be him behind my fortune, could it?

'No!' I got up and put a chair between us.

Magwitch smiled at his ruby red drink. 'Yes, Pip, dear boy, it's me wot done it! I swore each time I earned a pound, that the pound should go to you. I lived rough, that you could live smooth; I worked hard so that you could be above work. Do I tell you all this so you should feel in debt to me? Not a bit. I tell it, so you know that it was me, the hunted dunghill dog that you helped as a little boy – who went on to make a fortune so that he could make a gentleman – and, Pip, that gentleman is you!'

My legs went from under me and I collapsed back in my armchair.

Magwitch leaned closer. 'Look'ee here, Pip, I've lived a ramshackle life, I admit it, but I had a little daughter once. I loved her more than anything. But her mother was a violent woman. She only avoided a conviction for murder thanks to Jaggers's skill. That woman was mortal jealous of me if I so much as looked at another female. On the very night she was arrested for strangling a woman she'd seen me with – she swore to me that she would destroy our child ... ' His voice broke. 'That I would never see her again. My daughter vanished so she must've kept her oath. But you see, now I've a second chance. I'm your second father. You're my son – more to me than any son. Did you never think it might be me?' His eyes twinkled with glee.

'Never, never.'

Magwitch slapped his thigh. 'I expect there's some bright eyes somewhere, eh? They'll be yours, dear boy, if money can buy 'em. It warn't easy, Pip, for me to leave Australia, nor yet it warn't safe. But I had to one day come see my boy and at last, I done it!'

He put aside his empty glass and rubbed his hands together. 'So, where will you put me?'

'To sleep?'

'Aye, I've been sea-tossed and sea-washed, months and months. I must be put somewhere.'

'You can have Herbert's room – he's away.'

'He won't be back, will he? For you see, I have to be careful.' Magwitch went to the window and looked out on the pavement below. 'My enemy is on my tail. Gentleman Compeyson betrayed me at our trial and will do so again if he gets the chance.'

'What do you mean?'

'I was sent for life. It's a sentence of death to come back.' With that he threw himself on Herbert's bed and was soon fast asleep.

For an hour or more, I remained too stunned to think; and it was not until I began to think, that I began fully to know how wrecked I was, and how the ship in which I sailed was gone to pieces.

Miss Havisham's intentions towards me, all a mere dream.

Estella, not designed for me.

The old lady had invited me to Satis House so I could be used for practice as she prepared Estella for her future of tormenting suitors with her coldness. I had meant nothing to either of them.

But the sharpest and deepest pain of all: I realized that I had left my honest old life with Joe for the false rich existence given to me by Magwitch. Puffed up with my own importance, I had dared to look down on my best friend, the man who stood head and shoulders above me in worth.

Part III
Chapter One

Herbert returned to find me still sitting by the ashes of our fire.

'My dear Pip, why the long face? I hope it isn't bad news from home?' he asked.

'Oh, Herbert, I wasn't expecting you back yet from Clara's. I'm afraid you can't go in your room.'

'Why ever not?'

'I ... er ... had an unexpected visit from my ... my Uncle ... um ... Provis and ... ' I crumpled: if I couldn't tell my good friend, whom could I tell? 'Oh, Herbert, I am in such a tangle. I've discovered who my patron is – in there.'

Herbert peeped in.

'That's not Miss Havisham.'

'No. He says his name is Abel Magwitch. He's a convict returned illegally from Australia.'

'Ah.'

'I helped him as a boy and he dreamed of owning himself a gentleman.' I gave Herbert a mocking bow. 'I can't keep his money and keep my self-respect. His past is murky and violent, and it would surely involve me in his crime in the eyes of the law if I hid him and continued to profit from his wealth. But I am up to my ears in debt and I think Magwitch is in danger of being recaptured and put to death. And as to forming any plan for my own future, I could as soon as form an elephant!'

Herbert slumped into the chair Magwitch had occupied, even his optimism dented. 'That is quite a plateful of problems. But if I understand this right, you are his dream – if you cut the ground from under him suddenly, what might he do?'

'Something reckless.'

Herbert's energy was returning. 'Well, the first and main thing to be done is to get him out of England. We will continue to refer to him as your Uncle Provis to deflect suspicion.'

'But how are we going to persuade him to go when he's only just got here? He's risked so much to come and see the gentleman he made.'

'I fear you will have to offer to go with him for the moment. Then you can extricate yourself from the rest of the problems later once he is safe.'

'The case is urgent. He says he's tracked by another man, one Compeyson. I saw them fighting each other out on the marshes when I was little. They have a deadly feud.'

Herbert sat up. 'Compeyson? Are you sure he gave that name?'

'Yes. Do you know the fellow?'

'You remember I told you about the so-called gentleman who tricked Miss Havisham out of so much money – him that was in cahoots with her brother?'

'Of course, I remember.'

'Compeyson: that was the name of the villain who professed to be Miss Havisham's lover. I heard he had a criminal associate; both were sent to the Old Bailey and both found guilty. No wonder your benefactor chose Jaggers as your guardian – Mr Jaggers must have defended him at his trial. That just goes to show that Jaggers knows everyone!'

This was beginning to make sense – the hidden connections that had brought us to this point. 'Magwitch is very bitter. He feels he unfairly bore the brunt of the blame, while Compeyson got off much more lightly. In Magwitch's view, it should've been the other way round as he was but a follower in the plot. They remain a serious threat to each other. We are all in danger of prosecution if Compeyson brings the law to our door. Magwitch cannot stay here.'

'No, Pip, he can't.'

I stiffened my backbone. 'So it is settled: I'll go abroad with Magwitch. Yes, that is for the best.'

Herbert patted my knee. 'We'll move him to my

Clara's first. She and her father live by the Thames so we can lodge your Uncle Provis there and wait for an opportunity to slip him out, row down the river and put him on board a steamship – that way we avoid being seen in the city.'

'Thank you, Herbert.' I gazed mournfully at the door to his bedroom. 'You know, he is not at all what I expected.'

Chapter Two

Before I could leave the country, I had one important matter to settle. My secret support of Herbert's career had to cease. I could no longer support him as I was to return Magwitch's money, but I owed it to Herbert to find someone else who could. That is why I caught the coach back to Satis House.

When I knocked on the door, I was astonished to find that it was Orlick who answered.

'You here!' I exclaimed. 'What about your job at the forge?'

'Aye, I'm here. You aren't the only one as can better 'imself. Joe don't hold nobody back.' Orlick blocked my way.

'I need to see Miss Havisham.'

'Ah, but does she need to see you? Ain't seen you round 'ere much. Old Joe and Biddy not seen you neither.'

'Out of my way. I didn't come here to talk to you.' I pushed past him and entered the house only to find that Miss Havisham already had guests. Bentley Drummle stood at Estella's side in Miss Havisham's presence. My heart sank to my boots to see that he was kissing Estella's hand.

'So we have an understanding, Estella?' Drummle asked.

I wasn't sure if I knew what was happening between them for Miss Havisham shook her head but Estella motioned her to remain silent.

'We do, sir,' said Estella.

Drummle bowed and marched out. He might have been surprised to see me in the doorway but was clearly pleased to have a chance to gloat.

Miss Havisham did not greet me with her usual composure, her hand fluttering on her chest. 'Mr Pip, we did not expect to see you here again. What brings you to Satis House?'

I glanced over my shoulder but Drummle was gone. 'Miss Havisham, Estella, I will not keep you long, but I have a few things that need to be said. First, it will not surprise you, it will not displease you to hear that I am as unhappy as you can have ever meant me to be, Miss Havisham. I have found out who my patron is, and it is not a happy discovery. I can't say any more as the secret is not mine, but another's.'

'Not your secret but another's,' echoed Miss Havisham. 'Well?'

'I came here first, I suppose, as a kind of servant, to gratify a want or a whim, and to be paid for it?'

'Aye, Pip, you did.'

Estella walked away as if uninterested in anything I might have to say.

'And that Mr Jaggers—' I continued.

'Mr Jaggers had nothing to do with it,' interrupted Miss Havisham. 'His being my lawyer, and his being the lawyer of your patron, is a coincidence. He holds the same relations towards numbers of people, and it might easily arise. Be that as it may, it did arise, and was not brought about by anyone.'

'But I fell into the mistake that you had given me the money, and you led me on, did you not?'

'Yes, I let you believe it.'

'Was that kind?'

Miss Havisham gazed at me in amazement. 'Who am I, for pity's sake, that I should be kind?'

I turned away. 'Yes, it was weak of me to expect kindness of you. But no matter. I do not matter. I come here on behalf of two others. First, Herbert Pocket – a generous and good relation of yours who should not be lumped in with all the others of your kin that have designs on your money. He deserves this kindness and he is of your blood.'

'And what of him?'

'I have been paying for his position at Clarriker's. I ask you to take over the responsibility of supporting

Herbert in his career without his knowledge until such time as he is established.'

'Why must it be done without his knowledge?'

'Because I secretly began the service myself, more than two years ago, and I don't want him to know. Why I have to stop now, I cannot explain. It is part of the secret which is another person's and not mine.'

Miss Havisham paused, considering. 'What else?'

I turned next to the girl who had haunted me so long. 'Estella. You know I have loved you long and dearly. I should have said this sooner, but for my long mistake that Miss Havisham was the one who gave me my fortune. It persuaded me to hope that she meant us for one another.'

Estella stood frozen, hands clenched by her sides.

'I know I have no hope that I shall ever call you mine. It would have been cruel in Miss Havisham, horribly cruel, to practise on the innocent understanding of a little boy, and to torture me through all these years with a vain hope, if she had reflected on the seriousness of what she did. But I think that she did not. I think that, caught up in her own suffering, she forgot mine.'

Miss Havisham put her hand to her heart and held it there.

Estella cleared her throat. 'These are feelings that I am not able to comprehend. You address nothing in my breast, you touch nothing there.' She touched her heart. 'I tried to warn you of this, did I not?'

'Yes, but I hoped you could not mean it. You are still young – surely it is not natural to be heartless at our age?'

Estella's expression did not soften. 'It is how I have been brought up. I am making an exception for you by telling you what I would never admit to another.'

I felt anger now for both her and me. 'But you cannot marry Bentley Drummle! It makes me wretched that you should encourage a man so generally despised as Drummle.' Estella shrugged. 'You know he has nothing to recommend him but money, and a ridiculous roll of aristocratic, dim-witted ancestors, don't you?'

'What of that?'

'I cannot bear that people should say, she throws away her graces and attractions on a mere boor.'

'I can bear it.'

'But I cannot bear that you gave him such looks and smiles this very night, such as you never give to me.'

'Do you want me to deceive and entrap you then?' she replied angrily.

'Do you deceive and entrap him, Estella?'

'Yes, him and many others – all of them but you.'

'Take care you are not the one being trapped! Do not let Miss Havisham lead you to this fatal step. Put me aside for ever – you have done so, I know – but marry some worthier person than Drummle.' I would have gone on my knees if I felt such pleas would have moved her.

'I am going to be married to him. Why do you blame Miss Havisham? It is my own decision.'

'Your own decision, Estella, to fling yourself away upon a brute?'

'On whom should I fling myself away? Should I fling myself away upon a man like you,' she gestured to me, 'who would soon come to feel that I brought nothing to the marriage? No warmth? No affection? There! It is done. I shall do well enough and so shall my husband. As to leading me into what you call this fatal step, Miss Havisham would have me wait, and not marry yet; but I am tired of the life I have led, and I am willing enough to change it. Say no more. We shall never understand each other.'

I despaired for her. 'Such a mean, such a stupid brute!'

'Don't be afraid of my being a blessing to him. I shall not be that. Come! Here is my hand. Do we part on this, you idealistic boy – or are you now a man? This will pass in no time. You will get me out of your thoughts in a week.'

'Out of my thoughts! Estella, can you not see that you are part of my existence, part of myself? You have been in every line I have ever read, since I first came here, the rough common boy whose poor heart you wounded even then.'

She shook her head, denying it.

'Since we first met, I have seen you everywhere I have looked – on the river, on the sails of the ships, on the marshes, in the light, in the darkness, in the wind, in the woods, in the sea, in the streets. Estella, to the last hour of my life, you will remain part of my character, part of the little good in me, and part of the evil, for it was in the hope of winning you that I made myself into the man I am. But now your marriage is separating us for ever, I will promise in future to think only good of you.'

Estella looked at me in wonder.

'Heaven bless you and forgive you.' I held out my hands. She hesitated but made no move to take them. Miss Havisham plucked at her gown but Estella tugged free, gathered herself and left us both with head held high.

'Estella!' groaned Miss Havisham. 'Why? Why choose Drummle, of all men? It is no use: she will not be moved from her decision. I bred that stubbornness in her.'

She was trembling, deeply shaken by her foster child's decision, but she had not forgotten my earlier request. 'Pip, I want to show you that I am not all stone. You said, speaking for Herbert, that you could tell me how to do something useful and good. How much will it take to help your friend?'

It was hard to remember Herbert when all my hopes had walked out of the door with Estella. 'Nine hundred pounds.'

'If I give you the money, will your mind be more at rest?'

'Much more.'

'Are you very unhappy now?'

'I am far from happy, but there are other reasons than the ones you know.'

Miss Havisham nodded. 'It is kind of you not to lay all the blame at my door. Is it true you are unhappy?'

'Too true.'

'Can I only help you, Pip, by helping your friend? Is there nothing I can do for you yourself?'

'Nothing. I thank you for the question, but there is nothing.'

'Are you still on friendly terms with Mr Jaggers?'

'Yes.'

She took some papers from her dressing table and wrote on them with a pencil. 'This is a letter telling him to pay you that money for your friend. My name is on the first page. If ever you can write under my name "I forgive her" though ever so long after my broken heart is dust – pray do it!'

I took the paper and kneeled beside her, gently taking her frail hands in mine.

'O Miss Havisham, I can do it now. I need forgiveness far too much to be bitter with you.'

She closed her eyes as if in pain. 'Oh what have I done? What have I done? Until you spoke to her today, and until I saw in you a looking glass that showed me what I once felt myself, I did not know what I had done.'

'Miss Havisham, you may dismiss me from your mind and conscience. But Estella is your responsibility since it was you who made her this way. If you can ever undo any scrap of what you have done in killing all softer feelings in her, it is far better to do that than spend your time regretting past mistakes.'

'But Pip, my dear, believe this: when Estella first came here … ' Miss Havisham broke off, caught up in memories. 'Jaggers brought her to me, you know – she's the daughter of a convict and a woman who strangled another in some wretched fight, but what did that matter to me?'

'That child was Estella?'

'She was a pretty little girl, picked out by Jaggers from among the many poor children whom he sees that need rescuing. You see, Pip, I thought I could do her good. I wanted to save her from misery like my own. At first I meant no more. But as she grew, and promised to be beautiful, I gradually did worse, and with my praises, and with my jewels, and with my teachings, and with this example of myself always before her as a warning, I stole her heart away and put ice in its place.'

A bitter mistake, I thought. 'Better to have left her a natural heart, even to be bruised or broken.'

Abruptly I turned to go, but thinking better of my anger, came back to take a kinder farewell. It was then I saw she had drifted too close to the fire, dusty wedding dress trailing. A great flaming light sprang up. In that same moment, I saw a whirl of fire blazing all about her. I dragged the great cloth from the table with the bride's cake – I dragged down the heap of rottenness, and all the ugly things that sheltered there. We were on the ground, struggling like desperate enemies, and the closer I covered her, the more wildly she shrieked and tried to free herself. The patches of tinder, that a moment before had been her faded bridal dress, fell in a black shower around us.

I cradled her in my arms, aware I had burns on my hands but they were nothing to hers. 'Miss Havisham? Miss Havisham? Oh heavens, send for the doctor, someone! Help her! Help her!'

'Pip?' she said faintly.

'Don't speak. The doctor will be here soon. You'll be all right, I promise. Please be all right.'

'Pip?'

'Yes?'

'Take the pencil and write under my name that you forgive me.'

Chapter Three

Leaving Miss Havisham in the care of her doctor, I returned to London and found Mr Jaggers and Wemmick together in their office. I had two purposes coming here: first, to secure the promised aid for Herbert; and secondly, after Miss Havisham's hints, I was hot on proving Estella's parentage.

My appearance, with my bandaged burns and my coat loose over my shoulders, worked in my favour as they were eager to hear the cause. After describing the recent events at Satis House, I set to my tasks. They both knew, of course, the truth about Magwitch, though they would admit nothing in this office, and I had already told them that I would take no more money from him.

'Mr Jaggers,' I announced, 'I have here Miss Havisham's letter instructing you to give nine hundred pounds to Mr Herbert Pocket.'

Mr Jaggers signalled for Wemmick to draw up the cheque. 'I am sorry, Pip, that we do nothing for you.'

'Miss Havisham was good enough to ask me if I needed money but I told her "No." I felt I deserved nothing from her, or from anyone else.

Jaggers frowned at my lack of self-interest. 'I should not have refused, if I had been you, but every man ought to know his own business best.'

Wemmick sighed at my failure. 'Every man's business is to gain portable property.'

I refused to let their Newgate attitudes sway my decision to stand on my own two feet from now on, so I changed the subject. 'I did ask something of Miss Havisham, sir. I asked her to tell me about her adopted daughter. I think you must have long suspected that Estella has been the focus of my poor dreams. Miss Havisham told me all she knew.'

Mr Jaggers stilled. 'Did she?'

'And I think I now know the identity of Estella's mother. So do you, for she lives under your roof and is employed as your housekeeper. I met her at the dinner you held for me and my friends.'

'Yes?' He said it in such a tone so as not to admit anything.

'What's more, I believe I know Estella's father. A certain acquaintance of mine – recently returned from Australia.'

'And on what evidence, Pip, does this man make this claim?'

'He does not make it – he does not even know that his daughter still lives.'

Mr Jaggers paced again. 'Hah! What item was it you were at, Wemmick, when Mr Pip came in?'

I was not to be brushed aside this time. 'Wemmick, I know you to be a man with a gentle heart.' Wemmick flinched. 'I have seen your pleasant home, and your old father, and all the innocent playful ways with which you refresh your business life. I entreat you to say a word for me to Mr Jaggers and ask that he be more open with me.'

Mr Jaggers and Wemmick looked at each other aghast.

'What's all this?' said Mr Jaggers. 'You with an old father and you with pleasant and playful ways?'

Wemmick looked down in embarrassment. 'Well! If I don't bring 'em here, what does it matter?'

Mr Jaggers smiled openly for the first time. 'Pip, this man must be the most cunning imposter in all London.'

Wemmick shuffled some papers. 'Not a bit of it! But if I am, I think you're another, sir. I shouldn't wonder if you might be planning to have a pleasant home of your own, one of these days, when you're tired of all this work.'

Mr Jaggers didn't deny the charge but turned back to me. 'Now, Pip, let me put this case. Suppose a violent woman charged with a terrible crime had an innocent girl child, a fact she told her lawyer, fearing a long spell in prison – or worse. Suppose that same lawyer, on her request, was entrusted to find a safe haven for said child and happened to know of an eccentric rich old lady looking to adopt.'

'I understand you perfectly,' I said solemnly.

'But I admit nothing.'

'Nothing,' echoed Wemmick.

'Put the case, Pip,' Mr Jaggers continued, 'that the mother's mind was shaken by the terror of death and when she was set at liberty, she went to her lawyer to be sheltered. Put the case that he took her in, and that he helped her control her old wild nature whenever he saw it breaking out. Now ask yourself, for whose sake would you reveal the secret of the child's parentage?' Mr Jaggers looked at me solemnly. 'For the father's?' he went on. 'He could not help the child. For the mother's sake? I think if she had done such a deed she would be safer where she was. For the daughter's? I think it would not be good if her new husband learned the truth. The news that she came from such parents would drag her back to disgrace. She has been free of that taint for twenty years; why spoil her future at a time when she must think she is safe for life? And while you are weighing up your decision, add that you love her, Pip. You have made her the subject of those "poor dreams" that have been in the heads of more men than you guess. I tell you, rather than tell her secret, it is better that you chop off that bandaged left hand and then pass the chopper to Wemmick there so he could chop off the bandaged right too!'

There was silence. Wemmick and I exchanged a look. Wemmick put his finger to his lips first, then I copied him, and finally Mr Jaggers repeated the gesture, agreement that Estella's parentage would remain a secret between us.

Mr Jaggers tapped the ledger. 'Now, Wemmick, what item was it you were at, when Mr Pip came in?'

I made to leave but lingered long enough to see a client enter.

Wemmick scowled at him. 'What are you about? What do you come snivelling here for, Mike?'

Mike circled his cap in his fingers. 'I didn't do it, Mr Wemmick.'

'How dare you? You're not in a fit state to come here, if you can't come here without crying like a leaking pen. What do you mean by it?'

Mike sniffed. 'A man can't help his feelings, Mr Wemmick.'

Jaggers pointed imperiously to the door.

'Now, look here, my man. Get out of this office. I'll have no feelings here. Get out.'

Mike obeyed quickly.

Wemmick slammed the door behind him. 'It serves you right. Get out.'

Jaggers and Wemmick nodded at each other, pleased at this little piece of hard-heartedness, their rhythm restored.

Chapter Four

The day for moving Magwitch dawned. I looked out the window of Clara's house at the twinkling lights upon the bridges of the Thames. The sun was coming up like a marsh of fire on the horizon. The river flowed dark and mysterious. As I gazed at the clustered roofs, with the church towers and spires shooting into the unusually clear air, the sun rose, a veil seemed to be drawn from the river, and millions of sparkles burst out upon its waters. It was time to head for the boat.

Herbert stopped on the doorstep to kiss his sweetheart. 'Our thanks, Clara, for looking after Uncle Provis. I'll be gone a day or two. We'll run down with the tide to below Gravesend and hail the steamer for Hamburg.'

'Look after Herbert for me, Clara?' I asked, much comforted that I was leaving my friend in such good hands as I went abroad with Magwitch.

'I will, Pip, if he'll let me.' Clara kissed my cheek in farewell.

Herbert, our good friend Startop and I pushed out our boat with Magwitch as our passenger and we began to row downriver to meet with the steamer. Old London Bridge was soon passed and the White Tower and Traitors' Gate.

I marvelled that Magwitch sat peacefully on his

bench, seemingly unworried that we might be pursued. 'Magwitch, I think you are the least anxious of us all!' I said.

He folded his arms across his chest. 'If you knowed, dear boy, what it is to sit here alonger my dear boy in the sunshine, after having been day by day betwixt four walls, you'd envy me. But you don't know what it is.'

'Oh, I think I know the delights of freedom.'

'Ah, but you don't know it equal to me. You must have been under lock and key to know it equal to me – and I ain't a-going to spoil it by being anxious.'

'If all goes well, you will be perfectly free and safe again.'

'Dear boy! But we can no more see to the bottom of the next few hours, than we can see to the bottom of this river.' He dipped his hand in the river and smiled wistfully. 'We can no more control what will happen than I can hold on to this.'

Night was fast falling. We rowed on, speaking little, for four or five dull miles. What light we had seemed to come from the river rather than the sky, as the oars in their dipping struck at a few reflected stars.

At this dismal time we all came to the same conclusion: we were being followed.

'Was that a ripple?' asked Startop.

'Nay, just the wind,' said Herbert, but he didn't seem convinced of the fact.

I squinted into the darkness. 'Is that a boat yonder?'

'Where? I can't see,' said Herbert – but then we all saw the boat closing in. 'O Lord, they're heading right for us!'

We could now see that there was an officer and soldiers in the other vessel.

'Halt!' shouted the officer. 'You have a returned convict there. I call on him to surrender.'

Meanwhile, Magwitch had spotted his old enemy in the other boat. 'Compeyson!' he bellowed.

Startop was the first to realize that we had a new and far more serious problem. He pulled me around. 'Look, Pip – the Hamburg steamer!'

The steamship was almost upon us. 'Pull for shore – they'll run us down!' I shouted.

There was confusion on board the steamer as the crew saw the two little boats in their path. They called to us – gave the order to stop the paddles – but it was too late. The hull of the steamship struck our boats, tossing us all in the water. On the very second of impact, I saw Magwitch leap for the other boat and grab his enemy.

'Compeyson! If I'm going down, you're coming with me!' he yelled.

I lost sight of them as I went under. I seemed to struggle

with a thousand mill weirs[2] and a thousand flashes of light. I felt pure white terror. I was sinking – sinking. But then, miraculously, I kicked for the surface and got free of the river's drag. Surfacing not far from the bank, I swam to the little beach.

Staggering onto the shore, I looked desperately about for my friends.

'Herbert? Startop?' I called.

'Here, Pip.' Herbert appeared, helping Startop up the bank.

I could see no sign of my convict. 'Magwitch! Abel! Where is he?'

The officer stood upright, water puddling at his feet, scanning the river, while his men clambered to dry land around him. 'All are accounted for except the two convicts. I saw both men go under the path of the steamer. There's no hope.'

'No, no, look there!' I had spotted something in the water.

Wading back into the river, Herbert and I pulled Magwitch to the bank. He was still breathing. Compeyson did not surface. Losing no time, the officer ordered that chains be put on Magwitch.

---

[2] A mill weir is a dam next to a water-powered mill.

'Do you have to do that now? The man's half drowned!' I protested.

'It's my duty, sir.'

'What of Compeyson?' asked Herbert.

The officer shook his head.

I kneeled by Magwitch.

'Dear boy. I believe – I went under the steamer – and struck my head. My chest.' He was having difficulty breathing. 'We went down fiercely – Compeyson and me – locked in each other's arms. We struggled, but I got free, struck out and swam away.'

He looked to me to confirm his account. I did not know if it was the truth but it was what Magwitch wanted me to believe and I owed him that much. 'I don't doubt you.'

'Ah, Pip! I've seen my boy and he can be a gentleman now without me.'

'I will never stir from your side.'

Magwitch patted my cheek.

I held his hand there. 'You've been a much better man to me than I have been to others,' I told him. 'I pray that I will be as true to you as you have been to me.'

Chapter Five

As a returned convict, Magwitch had to face another trial. It was very short and very clear. Mr Jaggers represented him to the best of his ability.

'M'lud, I would mention before the court that the accused has taken to industrious habits, and has thrived lawfully and reputably in the place of his exile,' said Jaggers. 'Through honest toil and hard work he has become a man of considerable wealth.'

The judge was not impressed. 'That's all very well, Mr Jaggers, but nothing can change the fact that he has returned illegally, for I see the man standing here before us. It is impossible to do otherwise than find him guilty.'

The judge turned to Magwitch as he stood in the dock. 'The appointed punishment for his return to the land that cast him out, being death, and him being an extremely serious case, I must bid the prisoner to prepare himself to die.'

Magwitch heard the verdict with resignation. 'My lord, I have received my sentence of death from the Almighty, but I bow to yours.'

As Magwitch suspected, the injury he had taken in the river acted more swiftly than the law. His health failed rapidly while waiting in prison for his sentence to be carried out. I kept as much as possible to his side as I now saw in him a man who had been a better friend to me than I had been to Joe.

'Are you in much pain, Abel?' I asked.

'I don't complain of none, dear boy,' he replied gruffly.

'You never complain.'

'Ah, but you've been more at ease with me, since I was under a dark cloud, than when the sun shone. That's best of all.'

I blinked back tears. 'Dear Magwitch, I must tell you something. You understand what I say?'

Magwitch squeezed my hand.

'You told me once that you had a child – a little girl whom you loved but thought lost. Remember? Well, she's not lost. I traced her for you. Mr Jaggers took the mother in – she's safe too. But your daughter, oh your daughter: she found powerful friends. She is a lady now, to be wed to a ... fine gentleman, and she's very beautiful.'

'My daughter – my own blood – a lady? Well, blow me down.' His voice was but a whisper.

'Yes, a lady – and the finest you ever did see. And I love her.'

His head dropped quietly onto his breast – and he died.

Chapter Six

Magwitch's death ended the chapter of my time as a rich gentleman, yet life for my other friends carried on improving. With Miss Havisham's secret support, Herbert was promoted to the position of partner in his firm and, ignoring his family's objections, was able to marry his Clara. They moved to Cairo to manage Clarriker's office there. Even Wemmick moved on with his personal plans. He called on me one day, carrying a fishing rod on his shoulder.

'I know you are out of sorts, Mr Pip, but I'm going to take a walk. More than that; I'm going to ask you to take a walk with me.'

I rose slowly from my couch, wracked by a fit of coughing. I had not been well since nursing Magwitch in prison. 'I'd be happy to, but I am not fit for a fishing expedition.'

Wemmick smiled. 'Never mind that.'

My curiosity was roused by his mysterious manner. 'Where are we going, Mr Wemmick?'

'You'll see soon enough, Mr Pip.'

As we approached Walworth, he took a diversion from the usual road to his house.

'Halloa! Here's a church! Let's go in.' When we

entered, he put down his rod. 'Halloa! Here's two pairs of gloves! Let's put 'em on.'

I now saw that the aged parent escorted in a blushing Miss Skiffins in her best bonnet.

'Halloa! Here's Miss Skiffins!' cried Wemmick. 'Let's have a wedding. Halloa, my dear.'

The vicar entered and began the service, speaking up at the shouted request of the aged parent. The priest reached the part of the blessing of the ring and looked up expectantly.

'A ring? Fancy that!' Wemmick patted his pocket. 'Halloa, here's a ring!' He put it on Miss Skiffins's finger. 'Thank you, vicar.' Wemmick picked up his rod again. 'Now, Mr Pip, let me ask you whether anybody would imagine this to be a wedding party?' I shook my head. 'I thought not.' He sounded very pleased with himself.

'Mr Wemmick, *Mrs* Wemmick, I wish you joy,' I said.

'Thankee!' Wemmick took me aside. 'She's such a skilled manager of chickens. You shall have some eggs and judge for yourself.' I turned to go but he caught me. 'I say, Mr Pip! This is altogether a Walworth sentiment, please, not one I would voice in the office, you understand.'

'I understand,' I replied solemnly.

'After what you let out the other day, Mr Jaggers must not know of it. He might think my brain was softening.'

As the expectations of my worthy friends rose, mine sank. I succumbed to my fever and, at this lowest point in my fortunes, I was arrested for debt. No money – no friends – or so I believed. As I lay ill in Newgate debtors' prison, rambling in my delirium, I thought I saw Joe at my side.

'Is it Joe?'

'Aye, old chap.' Joe sat on a little stool, heating soup over my meagre fire.

'Oh Joe, you break my heart! Be angry with me, Joe. Tell me of my ingratitude. Don't be so good to me!'

'Ah, Pip, old chap. You and me were ever friends, Pip. And when you're well enough we're going out for a ride – what larks, eh?'

'How long, dear Joe?'

'You meantersay, Pip, how long have your illness lasted?'

'Yes, Joe.'

'Well, tomorrow is the first of June.'

Weeks had passed. 'So long? And have you been here all that time, dear Joe?'

'Pretty nigh, old chap. We 'ad a letter from a man named Wemmick saying as how you might be amongst strangers, and that how a visit at such a moment might not prove unacceptabobble. And Biddy's word were,

"Go to him without loss of time." That were the word of Biddy.'

I felt safe for the first time in many days. 'Dear Biddy. What news of home? Miss Havisham? Did she survive her injuries from the fire? Is she dead?'

'Why you see, old chap, I wouldn't go as far as to say that, for that's a deal to say; but she ain't ... '

'Living, Joe?'

'That's closer to where it is. She ain't living.'

'Did she linger long?'

'About a week after you took ill.'

'Dear Joe, have you heard what becomes of her fortune?'

'It do appear that she had settled the most of it on Miss Estella.' He brought me a cup and helped me sip, distracting me from my grim surroundings with news from home. 'And Orlick, 'im that worked for me and was 'er gatekeeper, he's been arrested for breaking into Pumblechook's cash box. What was worse, 'e and 'is gang slapped Pumblechook's face and pulled his nose, tied 'im up to his bedpost, and stuffed his mouth full of flowerin' annuals to prevent 'im cryin' out! Orlick's now under suspicion of attackin' Mrs Joe—'

'Oh Joe!'

'Aye, seems 'e boasted of it to 'is gang. He's in the

county jail. A bad lot, that 'un. Seems I was wrong about 'im.' Joe tugged at his collar. 'Oh, and I ... er ... married Biddy.'

I hid my shock but lately I had been counting on the fact that Biddy would still be there waiting for me after all my mistakes. 'Dear Joe. I wish you both happiness. You have the best wife in the world then.'

'I'll stay here as long as you need me.'

And he did. But whether Joe knew how poor I was, and how all my great expectations had all dissolved, like our own marsh mists before the sun, I do not know. Maybe he did, for when I had recovered, I went to find him but he had already gone, leaving only a note and a receipt cancelling my debt, thus opening the doors of my prison.

I sold all I had to pay off the rest of what I owed and went out to join Herbert in Cairo. I became a clerk for Clarriker and Co. Many a year went round before I was a partner in the house; but I lived happily with Herbert and his wife, and lived frugally, and paid my debts, and maintained a constant correspondence with Biddy and Joe. It was not until I became the third in the firm that Mr Clarriker revealed my own part in Herbert's partnership. Herbert was much moved and amazed.

Eleven years passed before I returned to the forge to

find Joe and Biddy and another little Pip sitting by the fire. Though a little older, both looked very much the same as I remembered them, happy and content in their chosen life.

'We gave him the name of Pip for your sake, dear old chap,' said Joe. 'We hoped that he might grow a little bit like you, and we think he do.'

I was touched by their faithful love for me over the years. 'Biddy, you must give Pip to me, one of these days; or lend him, at all events,' I said.

Biddy refused to hear that I intended to remain childless. 'No, no, you must marry.'

'So Herbert and Clara say, but I don't think I shall, Biddy. I am already quite an old bachelor.'

She gave me an understanding look. 'Dear Pip, you are sure you don't fret for her?'

'Oh no – I think not, Biddy.'

'Tell me as an old friend. Have you quite forgotten her?'

'My dear Biddy, I have forgotten nothing. But that poor dream has all gone by. I wonder what became of Estella?'

'They say she had an unhappy marriage. Her husband died though, some two year ago after a fall from his horse. He whipped it too hard and tried to take a fence it could not manage. Both horse and master died. For all I know, she could be married again. She's not been seen about these parts.'

News of these sad events turned my thoughts to Miss Havisham's old place. 'Maybe I'll take a walk to Satis House now. For old times' sake. Put some ghosts of my past to bed.'

'Aye, you do that, Pip. I'll get supper ready for you while you're gone.'

Joe patted me on the shoulder. 'Don't be long Pip. It seems so long since we 'ad you all to ourselves; I don't want to waste a moment of your holiday. Such larks, Pip, Little Pip, such larks!'

And so I set out. A cold shivery mist veiled the afternoon, and the moon was not yet up to scatter it. But the stars were shining beyond the mist, and the moon was coming, and the evening was not dark. I was looking along the desolate garden walk when I beheld a solitary figure.

'Estella!' I hurried to catch up with her.

She stood still, waiting for me to reach her. 'I am greatly changed. I'm surprised that you know me.' The freshness of her beauty may have dimmed, but she still was majestic to my eyes. And for the first time, as we shook hands, I felt her touch was friendly.

I led her to a bench and we sat side by side. 'After

so many years, it is strange that we should meet like this, Estella, here where we had our first meeting. Do you often come back?'

She gazed around the bleak garden. 'I have never been back here since she died.'

'Nor I. Poor old place.'

'You are wondering how it came to be in this condition?'

'Yes, Estella.'

'It's the only possession I've not given up. Everything else was taken from me, little by little, but I have kept this. It was the subject of the only determined resistance I made in all the wretched years I was married.'

'Is it to be built on?' I asked.

'Yes, at last. I came to take leave of it. I had heard you live abroad. Do you still?'

'Still. In Cairo with Herbert.'

'And do well, I am sure?'

'I work pretty hard but earn enough, and therefore – yes, I do well.'

She folded her hands on her lap. 'I have often thought of you.'

'Have you?'

'Of late, very often. There was a long, hard time when I refused to remember what I had thrown away when I was quite ignorant of its worth. But, since I am now widowed and am free to think of one who loved me, I have given you a place in my heart.'

'You have always held your place in my heart.'

'I little thought I should say goodbye to you at the same time as saying farewell to this house. I am very glad to do so.'

'Glad to part again, Estella? To me, parting is a painful thing. I have always regretted how we last parted.'

'But you said to me, "Heaven bless you and forgive you!" And if you could say that to me then, you will not hesitate to say that to me now – now, when suffering has been stronger than all other teaching, and has taught me to understand what your heart used to be. I have been bent and broken, but – I hope – into a better shape. Be as considerate and good to me as you were, and tell me we are friends.'

'We are friends.' I offered my hand.

'And will continue friends apart,' said Estella.

I took her hand in mine, and we went out from that ruined place. The evening mists were rising now, and in all the broad expanse of tranquil light, I saw the shadow of no parting from her.

Nineteenth-century Justice

Magwitch is one of Charles Dickens's great characters. We meet him at the start of the story, just after his escape from a prison ship. In the nineteenth century criminals really were kept on prison ships, awaiting transportation to Australia. This was an easy and cheap way of removing people who committed crimes from society. Conditions on these old vessels, also known as hulks, were dreadful – disease spread and many prisoners died.

Convicts who were transported faced a long and uncomfortable journey. It could take six months to sail to Australia, and the convicts were kept below deck for the entire journey, cramped and sometimes chained up. The convicts who were sent away were not necessarily hardened criminals – one 70-year-old lady was transported for stealing some cheese!

After arriving, the convicts would most probably have found their new life far from home difficult. However, conditions improved by the mid-nineteenth century and many convicts led successful lives after they had served their time, just as Magwitch does in this story. Transportation changed their lives forever, as it did Magwitch's ... and Pip's too.